Sunny Numbers

A Florida Counting Book

Written by Carol Crane

Illustrated by Jane Monroe Donovan

Sleeping Bear Press
310 North Main Street
P.O. Box 20
Chelsea, MI 48118
www.sleepingbearpress.com

Printed and bound in Canada.

10 9 8 7 6 5 4 3 2 1

Library of Congress Cataloging-in-Publication Data on file.
ISBN:1-58536-050-3
Crane, Carol, 1933-
Sunny numbers: a Florida counting book / written by Carol Crane ;
illustrated by Jane Donovan.
p. cm.
Summary: Various objects, animals, and people associated with the state of
Florida are presented in short rhymes, with added commentary, and used
to illustrate counting, multiplying, and adding.

Counting—Juvenile literature. 2. Florida—Juvenile literature.
 [1. Counting. 2. Multiplication.
3. Addition. 4. Florida] I. Donovan, Jane (Jane Monroe) ill. II. Title.

QA113 .C73 2001
513.2'11—dc21

2001042894

1 Old Lighthouse
    warning those at sea.
        Stay away, the rocks are close,
            sail away from me.

Florida's first lighthouse was built to protect the nation's oldest seaport at St. Augustine. Twice, in 1824 and 1874, lighthouses were built at St. Augustine. Many storms caused the land under the first lighthouse to give way. The second lighthouse still exists. It can signal ships up to 24 miles away. Painted with black and white barber-pole stripes, it can also be seen by ships in the daytime. Through the years many families have lived and kept the light burning in the St. Augustine lighthouse. There are many wonderful books about brave light-keepers and their children. The lighthouse is now maintained by the U.S. Coast Guard.

1

The Sunshine Skyway Bridge is a marvel to look at day or night. The two support towers are gold in color and can be seen by both ships and car passengers. The bridge crosses Tampa Bay, a large body of water used by barges and freighters from all over the world. If the bridge were not in place, cars would have to travel 50 miles around Tampa Bay. Now, with this beautiful bridge, the trip across the bay is only 15 miles.

2 Support Towers
holding up the Skyway Bridge.
Cars travel over, boats sail under,
built so there is no drawbridge.

3 Sailboats catching the wind,
trying to win the race.
The one with the red sail
setting the fastest pace.

Sailing is one of the fastest growing sports in Florida. There is more ocean shoreline in Florida than in any other state except Alaska. Many races are only 2 or 3 miles long, but some are hundreds of miles.

The beautiful sails on the boats look like butterflies dancing on top of the water, tipping and gliding along.

Have you ever taken a trip with your family and asked, "Are we there yet?" If you get out a map of Florida and trace the main highways with your finger, you may find that your trip will go a little faster. It is not unusual to have 4 U.S. Interstate Highways in a state. It is unusual to have 4 Interstate Highways end in a state. Florida is a peninsula, so Interstate Highways I-75 and I-95 end in Miami. I-10 ends in Jacksonville. I- 4 travels across the state starting at the Gulf of Mexico and ending on the east coast. How many miles have you traveled on a major Interstate Highway?

Gulf of Mexico

4 U.S. Interstate Highways—
these roads begin or end here.
Visitors, families, and friends,
traveling to see someone dear.

Apalachicola
Natural Forest

Osceola
National Forest

Ocala
National Forest

Everglades
National Forest

INTERSTATE
95

INTERSTATE
4

Atlantic Ocean

Starfish can be many different colors. They can be red, orange, yellow, brown, tan, pink, olive, or black. They use their arms to look for food. They eat clams, oysters, snails, and any soft mollusk they can get out of its shell. If you look at a starfish closely, you will see little holes in the spiny or bumpy part of its upper body. It pumps water through these holes to move about and gather food. Some starfish are very small, but some can be 20 inches in length.

5 Starfish
found along the shore.
5 Arms to help them walk
upon the ocean floor.

Since the 1500s, this beautiful horse has been a breed of royalty. Born with a coat dark gray, brown, or black in color, the horse's coat slowly turns a dazzling white. The horse is trained to be a graceful, "dancing" performer. Myakka, Florida has a winter training facility for these horses. To see them trot, dance, jump, and nod when the music starts is a wondrous event.

6 Lipizzan Horses
        acting like white knights.
When the music starts to play,
        they dance in the spotlight.

6

If you were in Tarpon Springs, Florida, the first thing you would see on the water is a sponge boat. This city is called the "Sponge Capital of the World." Many years ago, families from Greece moved to this area to continue their work diving for sponges to sell. They wear deep-sea diving suits and go into the water to the sponge beds. Sponges are invertebrates. This means they have no backbone. They have no mouth or body organs, but are still considered to be an animal. Sponges are very soft and are used to clean windows and cars. Sponges can be red, orange, or brown in color.

7 Tan Sponges—
divers go down and down,
bringing them up in baskets,
"Sponges For Sale!" in town.

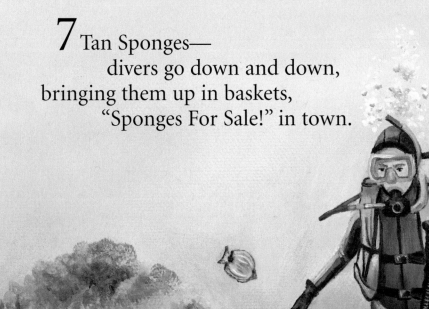

8 Long-Armed Octopi
escaping danger in a wink.
Hiding under coral reefs,
releasing a purple-black ink.

The Octopus is found in the waters all along Florida. It is a strange-looking creature with its pop-out eyes and 8 long arms with suckers for catching food. It can change its skin color using 3 pouches containing different colors of fluid. The different colors change with the octopus's mood—white for fear, and red for anger. Brown is its natural color. The Common octopus, found off the coast of west Florida, lays 200,000 to 400,000 eggs a year. Only 2 will grow up to be an adult.

8

9 Baseball Players
throwing and hitting the ball.
Practicing in the sun,
hearing the umpire's loud call.

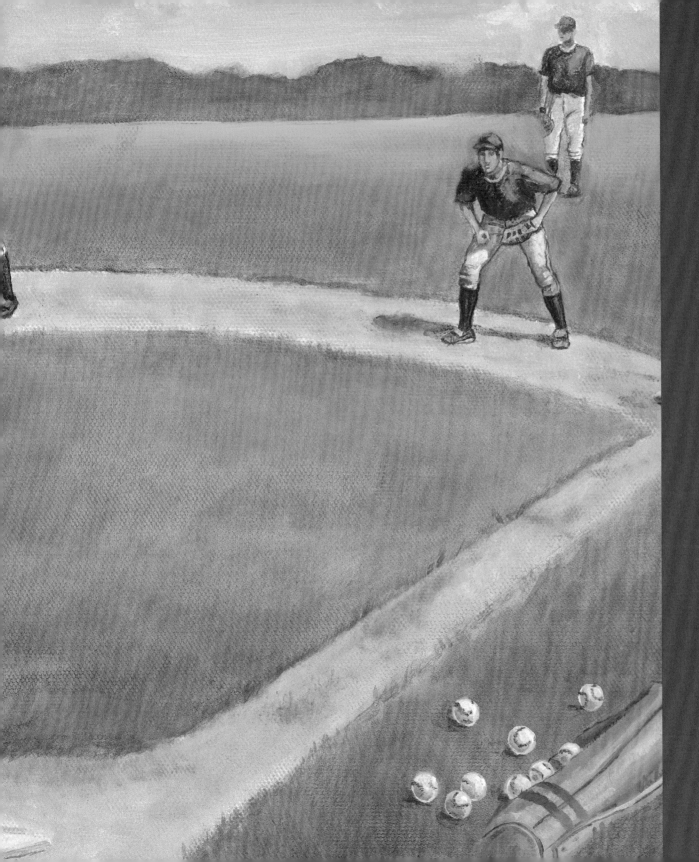

In February, when it is still cold and snowy in the North, baseball spring training starts in Florida. Beautiful stadiums, with flags flying and fans cheering, host the players until April when more than 20 professional teams head to their home cities all over North America. The warm and sunny weather has helped teams ready their players since before World War I. When peanuts, popcorn, cracker jacks, and hot dogs are sold, you know you're at the "old ball game."

9

Sand Dollars are beautiful to look at. It is hard to imagine that at one time they were living sea creatures. If you walk along the beaches and pick them up and clean them, they can be used as Christmas tree ornaments, necklaces, or window hangings. The tops have 5 slits and 5 petal flowers. On the underside center of the sand dollar is a set of 5 teeth. These are used for scraping algae off rocks, which is food for the sand dollar. Often, if you shake the sand dollar after it has dried, you can hear the old teeth rattle.

10 Sand Dollars
bleached by the sun.
I lay them on the beach,
and count them one by one.

Hernando DeSoto sailed from Havana, Cuba for Florida with 600 soldiers. He was sent by the King of Spain to claim the land and find gold. They looked for 4 years along the Gulf of Mexico, Texas, Arkansas, and also north along the Mississippi River. Along the way, they met hostile natives and were in many ambushes and wars. There were few soldiers left. Finally, sick and having found no treasure, DeSoto died. He is recognized today with a memorial near Bradenton, Florida as one of the early explorers of the Gulf Coast.

11 Spanish Explorers,
rowing to the shore.
DeSoto's men were hopeful
to find gold and more.

11

Silver Springs, Florida has a wealth of history. The Timucuan and Seminole Indians lived in this beautiful area called Ocali. Silver Springs is a natural wonder, with crystal clear waters that gush forth at the rate of 550 million gallons of water each day. Glass bottom canoes were put into use in 1878. Since then, larger glass bottom boats are available for viewing fish, turtles, crustaceans, and fossils. In the 1930s, a troop of wild Rhesus monkeys was established on an island in the Silver River. The monkeys were excellent swimmers and quickly escaped, forming wild troops along the river. Two years later, 6 of the original Tarzan movies were filmed on location in Silver Springs. Maybe some of these monkeys became stars too! The beauty of the location brought other filmmakers to the area. Such films as "The Yearling" and "The Creature from the Black Lagoon" were produced here. Also, 100 episodes of the TV show "Sea Hunt" were filmed here.

12 Wild Monkeys,
brought to a Silver River Isle,
imported from the jungles,
seen by boaters once in a while.

12

Now we've counted to 12,
so let's try multiplying by 1.
Then we'll try, our 2s, 3s, and 4s,
until we are all done.

1 x 1 = 1 Lighthouse

1 x 2 = 2 Support Towers

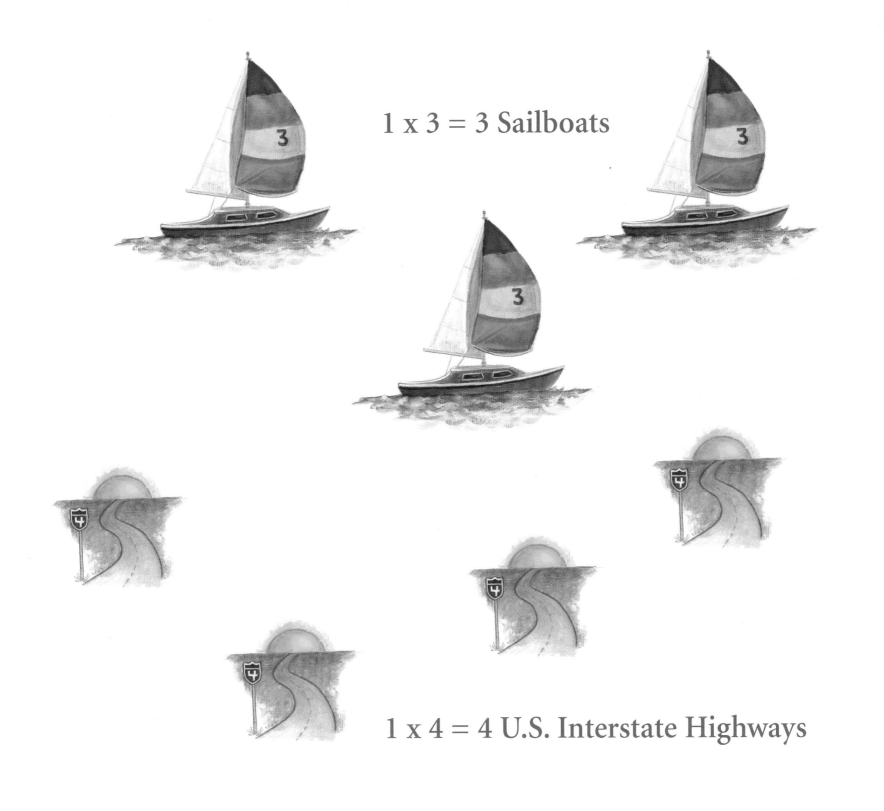

1 x 3 = 3 Sailboats

1 x 4 = 4 U.S. Interstate Highways

The Black Bear family loves to find honey. Florida is the number one honey-producing state, so bears can often cause beekeepers a lot of trouble. A single bear can tear apart dozens of hives to get at the honey inside. Florida Black Bears do not hibernate as long as their northern cousins, so they are often a threat to the bees and honey all year long. Bears are Florida's largest land mammals. The mother bear usually has 2 cubs. She teaches her cubs for 18 months and then they are on their own. Bears also like berries, insects, hearts of cabbage palm, and tender hearts of saw palmetto. They love to swim and will stay in the cool water during the hot summer.

2 x 1 = 2 Black Bears

2 Black Bears
climbed up a tree.
Mothers looking for honey,
and stung by a bee.

2 x 2 = 4 Marsh Rabbits

4 Marsh Rabbits
  walking through the bog.
Hear an alligator coming,
  jump up on a log.

Marsh Rabbits love to swim. In the swamps, they keep their bodies underwater and only their nose and eyes are visible. Swimming helps them survive in their marshy habitat. Marsh Rabbits walk instead of hopping like other rabbits. Sometimes, these rabbits even walk on their hind legs.

Wild pigs are also called wild hogs, razorbacks, or piney woods rooters. Pigs were brought to Florida from Spain by explorer Hernando DeSoto to feed his soldiers. The wild pigs found in Florida today are a mixture of wild boars and farm pigs that roam free.

They are black or dark brown in color and some are even spotted. They live near water, as they cannot tolerate the hot weather. They are often found in mud, swamps, or riverbeds trying to stay cool. They eat everything in sight. Mother pigs have 5 to 12 piglets. Wild pigs have dangerous 2-inch teeth that are razor sharp. They will use these teeth to protect their young.

6 Wild Pigs—
babies and their mother.
Looking for food to eat
to share with one another.

2 x 3 = 6 Wild Pigs

8 Armadillo Babies
are born in sets of 4.
Armored little diggers
their mother will adore.

2 x 4 = 8 Armadillos

In Spanish, Armadillo means "little armored one." These mammals have 9 bands of stiff bony plates. They have scaly rings on their tails and a shield protects their heads. Armadillos love to dig in yards, golf courses, and farmers' fields looking for insects. They have a very keen sense of smell. They can find insects underground, dig for them with sharp claws, and then scoop them up with a long sticky tongue. There are always 4 babies born to a mother armadillo.

Armadillos can cross a body of water by walking along the bottom as they hold their breath. They can also swallow air to inflate their stomachs to aid them in swimming across water.

There is nothing like a picnic with slices of chilled watermelon. Florida is one of the nation's top watermelon growers. Watermelons used to grow so large in Florida, they were hard to lift. Now, farmers are growing smaller varieties. With names like "Minilee" and "Mickeylee," some varieties sound like Florida attractions. Many farmers know how to grow seedless watermelons, but they don't seem to be as much fun to eat as the spitting-seed kind.

Now, we've tried multiplying,
let's read and try some more.
We did 1 and 2,
let's go to 3 and 4.

3 Juicy Watermelons
with seeds we spit so far.
Trying to win the contest,
and get them in a jar.

3 x 1 = 3 Juicy Watermelons

6 Pieces of Key Lime Pie
mother made for me.
It only takes 3 limes
picked off the fruit tree.

3 x 2 = 6 Pieces of Key Lime Pie

Key Lime Pie is often served with lots of whipped cream on top. Yum! Yum! The Keys in Florida are famous for their Key Lime Pie. However, most Key limes are grown in Mexico. They can be grown in Florida, but they like very warm, tropical weather. The limes are very hard to pick because they have thorny branches. The limes range in size from a golf ball to a ping-pong ball. The skin of the key lime is greenish yellow.

Imagine an orange so small you can hold 9 of them in your hand. The Kumquat shrub first came from China. The United States now grows this small fruit in Florida and California. You can pick Kumquats off the branches and pop them in your mouth, peel and all. Some are round in shape while others are oval. They are preserved in jams and syrups. How about white chocolate kumquat candy?

9 Orange Kumquats—
eat them peel and all.
Pop them in your mouth
for they are very small.

3 x 3 = 9 Orange Kumquats

3 x 4 = 12 Quarts
of Strawberries

12 Quarts of Strawberries,
plump red, juicy, and ripe.
Picked in the cool morning,
delicious eating type.

The Osprey is a large bird of prey. It easily swoops down into the water feet first and scoops up fish with its sharp talons. It has a white head like a bald eagle. This bird has white underneath its wings and body. It lives along waterways. If you are traveling along and see twigs and branches on top of telephone poles, it is usually an osprey nest. They are not afraid of cars or people, so they are able to live in areas that are busy with both.

4 x 1 = 4 Ospreys

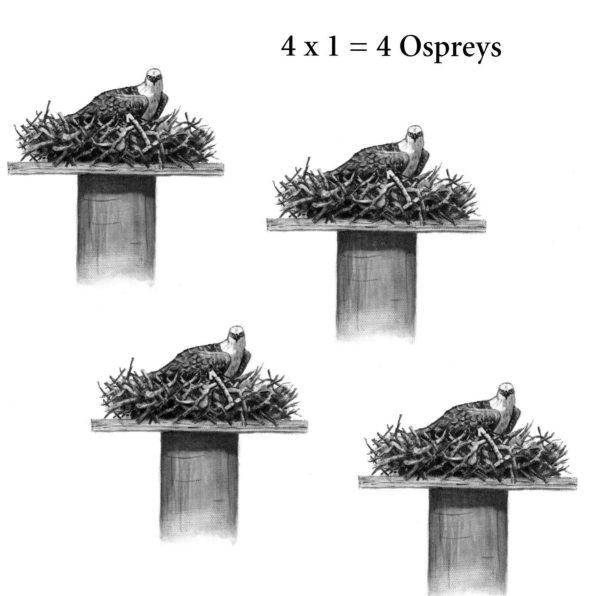

4 Osprey
sitting on their homes of branches up high.
Telephone pole nests along the road—
do you see baby birds as you go by?

8 Great White Heron
living in the Florida Keys.
Knees are on backwards,
    walking softly and wading free.

4 x 2 = 8 Great White Heron

This regal-looking white water bird is found mostly in the Keys or the Everglades National Park. It has pure white feathers and light-colored legs. When walking, it plops its large feet down slowly, as if it is in no hurry. A very large bird, it stands 4 feet tall and has a wingspan of 6 feet.

The Spanish explorers who came to Florida were very impressed by the Wild Turkeys. They took many of these birds to Spain. The Wild Turkey goes back in history to the days of the Pilgrims. Turkeys are very alert and can be challenging prey. Most birds that fly long distances have dark meat in their breasts. It takes more blood going through their breasts to stay in flight. Turkeys have more white meat in their breasts, as they often do not fly. The leg meat is very dark because they mostly walk or run. Sometimes, they will fly into a tree and roost to escape danger or to sleep.

12 Florida Wild Turkeys strutting in the woods. Thanksgiving is coming, finger-licking good!

4 x 3 =12 Florida Wild Turkeys

16 Cattle Egrets
looking for an insect morning snack.
It's so funny to see
white birds riding cattle's backs.

4 x 4 =16 Cattle Egrets

Hurricanes bring many birds to our states from other countries. Cattle Egrets were unknown in Florida until the 1930s. They came from Africa on the winds of a hurricane.

When riding through a cattle ranch, it is quite natural to see these white birds sitting on the cattle's backs. The movement of the cattle stirs up insects in the grass and the Egrets eagerly eat the bugs.

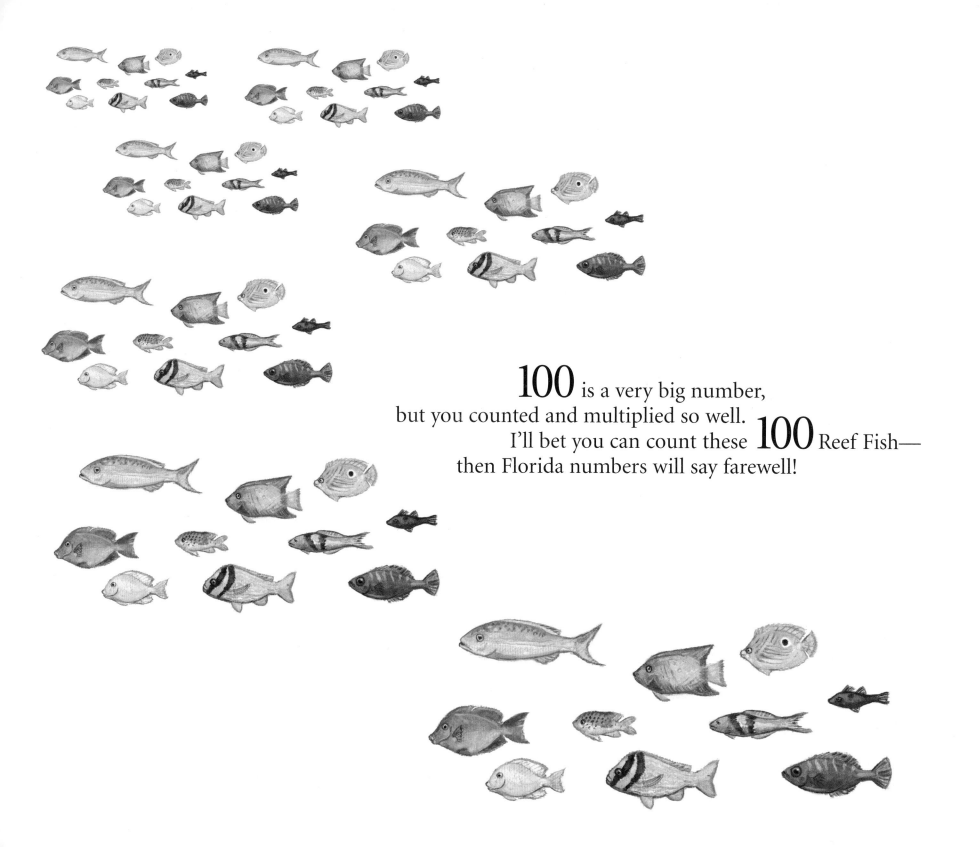

100 is a very big number,
but you counted and multiplied so well.
I'll bet you can count these **100** Reef Fish—
then Florida numbers will say farewell!

Carol Crane

Carol Crane has worked for 25 years reviewing, lecturing and enjoying children's literature. She is a nationally-recognized educational consultant, and has been a featured speaker at state and regional reading conventions across the United States.

Carol takes pride in writing children's books that are fun to read as well as educational. Her first title, *S is for Sunshine: A Florida Alphabet*, was published in the fall of 2000. She lives with her husband, Conrad, in Bradenton, Florida.

Jane Monroe Donovan

Jane Monroe Donovan enjoyed sketching as a child, and one of her best-loved gifts was a book of Norman Rockwell paintings given to her by her parents. She is a self-taught painter whose favorite subjects are people and nostalgic scenes.

She paints in a studio overlooking the pasture where her three horses graze, and when she's not painting she can be found riding through the woods with her Labrador retriever running alongside. Jane and her husband, Bruce, live in Pinckney, Michigan with their two sons, Ryan and Joey.